Become Credit Rich!

From Social Security S.S.I. to Credit Rich

Written by

Bishup Rich Wealth

ISBN: 978-1-959392-36-1

Dedication

I dedicate this book *Become Credit Rich* to my wife, Sarah Mensah, our children, and mother, Rose, and African families, working hard every day to have normal and better lives like everybody else in the world who has to obtain financial freedom for generations to come after me!

I also want to dedicate this book to Miss Scherryl Winston for being my second-greatest cheerleader to see me be successful like a money magnet.

Acknowledgment

I acknowledge Pastor David Crank of the Faith Church in St. Louis, MO. He was an inspiration to me, and one of his messages led me to this path; talking about how credit will make you rich if you know how to use it with discipline!

Contents

About the Author

From a very young age, I always wanted to make a lot of money to do the things I wanted to do without having to work for someone else.

As an author now, I have made this mini book available to the world to let you know there is a way to live a life of abundance and travel the world for yourself while blessing others with your generosity!

The answer is: BECOME CREDIT RICH!

Preface

Having a perfect or high credit score is something that we all dream of, but only a few are able to realize that dream. Building up your credit score can be a herculean task that most people have no clue about. They stumble and fall, trying to navigate and explore the world of credit.

Bishup Rich Wealth is a like-minded individual who wanted to have high buying power, just like his aunt. From an early age, he had seen how his aunt was able to buy him expensive things, all thanks to her high credit power. He, too, wanted this kind of power and so entered the world of credit. Unfortunately, he did not know of the complexities of credits and credit scores which soon landed him with a low credit score. Not being the one to easily give up, he got back on his feet and, through hard work, was able to become credit rich.

Chapter 1: Curious

My auntie Chilly always seemed so rich to me. After all, she could buy anything she wanted whenever she wanted, and she did not have to look at the price tag if she did not want to. I had no idea how she was buying these things and how she bought me a $1200 computer in early 2000 before she passed away in January 2016.

My auntie was amazing to me. I looked up to her because of her financial status and generous giving to friends and family mostly all the time. Auntie Chilly bought me a Roland keyboard six months later that cost $1000 to help me practice my music. I learned how to become my own music producer even though I didn't keep pursuing that dream at that time. But again, I was puzzled because auntie had spent nearly $2200 in that same year on gifts for me alone.

It did not seem like it fazed her at all. So, after seeing auntie prospering like this, I wanted to find out what it took for me to have the same buying power as her.

So now here's my Thuggamony from the T.h.u.g.g. Bishup.

In 2005, I went to a bank in Fort Wayne, Indiana, to start out with a secured credit card with $500. I was only cleared for that amount because my credit was bad. I do not know why I thought I could just walk into that bank and leave that day with a credit card. I really did not know what I was doing at the time, but I just knew that I wanted to be like Auntie Chilly; to buy whatever I wanted, when I wanted to, just like her.

I still did not know about a credit score just yet.

But I felt like the man with that $500 secured credit card. I took my wife shopping to buy new clothes and felt like a real millionaire swiping that card for the first time. I spent the whole $500 on my wife and never paid it off because we divorced soon after, and I moved out of town to Fort Worth, Texas, in 2006. As soon as I made it to Texas, I got with a bank that seemed like they were better than a credit card with their services. They would loan me up to $400 because I deposited my social security check with them each month's direct deposit. That turned out great for me for a whole year until I was ready to move to Dallas, Texas. Then I could not keep up the payments anymore because social security was my only income, and I needed that money to transition to my new apartment, so I left owing them a balance of $440 with interest.

Before I moved to Dallas, I went to court on February 27, 2006, and legally changed my name to Bishop. God was taking me somewhere with this whole thing with credit and my name change, and He would surprise me at the end of December that year. I never could get a credit card with my given birth name, Chris. But suddenly, when I changed my name legally to Bishop, a real credit card came in the mail unsecured for $200, and I had not even applied for it. I was ecstatic that this was happening to me. I spent that whole $200 like it was mine, but this time I would pay my first bill when it came in the mail. The first bill to that credit card was a $20 minimum payment to keep my credit card from being in default. Meaning to say not having a missed payment if you don't know what that means. Or I could pay whatever I want, or just pay off the whole bill of $200. I really thought I was the man for real now. I spent all $200 but only had to pay back a little portion without paying off the whole card.

I met a sister in Dallas who knew about credit, and she told me that I should not spend thirty percent on that card, or it could start messing up my credit. I wasn't trying to hear that because I thought I was doing just fine as long as I made the minimum payment and paid on time.

And just like I thought, after six months or more, the credit card company started asking me if I wanted a credit line increase that would give me more buying power. They would only extend it by another $100, allowing me to have $300, and after the credit line increased that year, I was at $1000 with them. The only thing was, even though I was extended to $1000, I never could enjoy spending that money on the card because I was at my limit with every credit line increase with them already.

A few months later, more credit card offers came in the mail, and I wasted no time applying for them. Unfortunately, they were all small limits of $400. So, I applied for two of them and started spending them up to the limit too, and would pay them on time with the minimum payment and made sure I was not late with them. I did not know what I was doing when I went to a credit union to get a secured loan from them. But when I found out how that worked. It blew my mind when I gave them $500, and then they put that money in a savings account, turned right around, and wrote me a $500 check after I gave them my $500.

But they explained that the next month I would start making $50 payments for the next 12 months until I paid back the whole loan and after I paid everything back to the bank. Then, they would give me back my $500. I wasn't asking any questions because I just left out of that credit union with the same $500 that I was coming to give them in the first place. But I didn't know that I was building my credit profile, which I would find out later. After having $1800 credit that was spent to the limit and just enough to buy little miscellaneous stuff back then, I stepped my game up in California. In 2011, I went to their mall, applied for a Kay jewelers credit card, and got approved for a credit card with them for a $400 credit limit.

I wasted no time once again buying something on it for $100. But at least I did not max out that card because I was not interested in wearing a bunch of jewelry, but I did make sure I was coming back the next month to pay their minimum payment too. That next month when I returned to that mall to pay Kay jewelers their minimum payment, I had to walk through a store called Macy's to get to them. A lady stopped me and asked me.

"Do you want to apply for a Macy's credit card?"

I immediately told her no. I did not think my credit was good enough for this name-brand store that was so hot in New York, where I was from. But she convinced me to apply when she told me that Sean Combs, better known as Puff Daddy, would be in that same mall the next month.

So all I had to do was get approved by them and buy Puff's perfume set called "Unforgettable" for $100 on my credit card. But that was only if I got approved, and I would be one of three hundred people to meet him in the mall in September 2011.

I had nothing to lose looking to meet the most famous Puff Daddy with this big vision and dream I had. So, I told her to run my credit and see what would happen. After one minute, she told me I was approved for $300.

I was so shocked. I hurried up to buy Puff's perfume kit to meet him. The rest of the Puff Daddy story is written in my book called *T.h.u.g.g. Journey part 2 Raw and Uncut* in the chapter called *Rubbing Shoulders with Fame* that you can purchase on Amazon for ten dollars as an e-book and the paperback book for $20.So now I had built my credit file up to $2500 and was still just paying the minimum payments on all five credit cards, making sure I was not late. So all five credit cards gave me $2500 between them, and then I would get another credit card blessing that I did not see coming. I was walking through Walmart when I was approached by another lady asking me to apply for a credit card.

"No problem," I said.

This stuff was getting easy for me after getting all these other credit cards.

I applied confidently, and after a few minutes, I was also approved for a $400 limit with them. Now my credit profile was up to $2900. But as soon as I received the card, I spent most of all my money buying food and paying the minimum payment. The next month when I went to the mall in Cali, I got approved for a JC pennies card for $500. Now I was thinking that my credit report was looking good at this time to get all of these credit cards back to back in such a short time. I wouldn't stop there after having this fun like this. There was a finance company in Tulsa, Oklahoma, that trusted me with $1200 when I visited them in February 2012. So now I started giving away gifts to women on my credit cards in different states that I had never met before but just talked over the chatline telephone to hear their voices. I felt so rich as I was still using up my limits on every credit card that I found out that was called maxing them out! I moved to California in 2011. Because of the cost of living in California, my social security check increased. I got an extra $200 added to my $700 to live on, more than what I would receive in the other states. I had extra money to balance out these credit card payments.

But this would only last for so long. I was only paying the minimum payments on those credit cards. I had an emergency in Fort Wayne, Indiana, with my mother Willa before she died in 2017, and I had to abandon California, which is written in the book chapter called *Burned up. "T.h.u.g.g. Journey part*

2 *Raw and Uncut"* on the Amazon website waiting for you to buy this powerful book for $10 as an E-book, and the paperback is $20! As soon as I left California, my social security check went back down to $700. Now I was in trouble for real because I did not have that extra $200 to keep up with all this bad debt I had attracted by being foolish and dumb with my spending habits with credit cards.

I was not feeling like a millionaire at this time. I felt like a dunce and a failure for being so careless and a bad steward using my credit cards! But I had to do something because I only had two options: pay all those minimum payments or be homeless. After all, I was not on a low income like I was paying for section 8 in California. I was about to throw away all my credit cards to have my whole social security check to live on without stressing about how I would keep up with these credit card payments. It did not take me long to figure out what to do next. I trashed every credit card and kept my sanity and peace.

Chapter 2: Bad Credit

I knew that I was at about a six hundred credit score before I threw away all these cards without paying them again, which made my credit score drop from 100 points to five hundred.

I was living a regular disability life again until God showed me how to start over again, and this time I would discipline my spending habits and learn the true ways of spending on a credit card.

This bad credit card stuff was not going to get the best of me with the new businesses that I had set up in Oklahoma when I moved to this state in 2013.

I was going to win, and I could not see any other way but to fix my credit with all these charge-offs now and derogatory marks that I would reed about on Credit Karma.

Chapter 3: Starting Over

God first showed me how to build positive credit over the negative credit that I had on my credit report. God showed me that if I did that in itself, I would start making my credit look better in due time.

I wasted no time. I went to a bank in Oklahoma City and started with a secured card with a $300 limit this time. But when it got to me, I fought my hardest not to spend over thirty percent and not to max out this credit card. Then I went to another bank which was in a Walmart where I lived and applied for a secured loan like before, and this time I understood that after that whole year, I should have better results with my credit report as I paid over the minimum payments and on time.

Now it's the year 2014, and I kept those payments way above the minimum this time. I even saved $100 each month for the next year to add to my credit card as a credit limit increase. This stuff worked because it took my credit score up to six hundred, and the derogatory accounts on my credit report fell off with help from a credit repair agency that I used for a few months.

I went to Lexington law, where they removed some accounts for me.

By 2015, I was creeping up the ladder again with my credit, even though I now had more than a little bit of negative history.

I took a chance to apply for a capital one business spark credit card and got approved for $1000.

You could not have told me that I wasn't the man on top again. For the next four years, I kept my credit cards in good standing, and after paying my cards on time and early, I stayed at less than what I was told to spend, thirty percent or lower. All of this took me to a credit score of seven hundred by the time I was moved into St. Louis, Missouri, in the year twenty nineteen.

God was about to blow my mind with my new bank. They really loved my credit score and saw that my capital one business card was built up to $3000 at this time.

Chapter 4: High Credit Limit

I spoke to my credit union, applied for one of their credit cards, and got approved for fifteen thousand dollars on the first wop. I was trippin'. I've never had any other bank want to reward me like this, and I knew that I could not mess this up for real.

God was really rewarding me for my discipline and how I have now learned to master these credit cards, put my flesh in check and try not to buy everything just because I could.

The pandemic rose on us by the end of 2019 and early 2020. But I did not let this stop me from being a good steward over this new large limit of credit that was given to me.

I spent so much on this card with Amazon to buy food and stay away from those getting sick and dying because of covid 19. I could pay my balance off quickly that year because I received a $7500 donation to the ministry in 2019, in the summer that I held on to until I got this larger amount of credit.

Six months passed with me having a perfect history with my new credit union, so I asked them for a credit limit increase. I was approved for four thousand dollars to add to the fifteen-thousand-dollar positive credit to make my credit at nineteen thousand dollars of positive credit, and before I could look up, as we say, I had a credit score of seven hundred and forty.

I thought Credit Karma was lying to me. Then I called the real credit bureau trans union to see if this was true, and they told me that I was higher than that at a seven fifty credit score.

Chapter 5: Credit Rich

After seeing myself climb the ladder like this, I applied for another credit card and was approved, this time for twenty-five thousand dollars. I am really becoming credit rich and able to be more of a blessing to other people in lack. This larger limit of credit would come in handy for some of the people I met on Facebook in Ghana, Africa, during this pandemic who were hurting and without jobs to take care of their babies and siblings because of the shutdowns in that country.

The first stimulus check came for twelve hundred dollars when President Donald Trump was still in office. I gave away that whole check to a family in Ghana to have shelter and food.

I felt so good that my credit allowed my non-profit organization, Changed People today INC., to help and give to the less fortunate than us in America.

I applied one last time with my credit union. I was approved for eighteen thousand dollars, which brought my positive credit to sixty-two thousand dollars, with the other credit cards I own with Discover, American Express, and Capital one personal cards with smaller limits. As you read this short story, I have built my credit report to positive seventy-three thousand dollars, and I'm at a perfect eight hundred credit score today.

I had one more thing that I wanted to see myself achieve but this time, not with a personal credit card. I applied in March 2022 to get approved with a business credit card because I needed a real business card that would not report to personal credit. They would only report to business credit profiles and would not lower my score for more significant purchases if I had to make them. They gave me eighteen thousand dollars, which has me at ninety-one thousand dollars positive credit.

The funny part about all this is that I manage all of this credit with a social security check once a month as my stable income that will come once a month for eight hundred dollars.

Thank you, Jesus, for you taught me how to win in the credit game, and become credit rich! LOL

Instructions in This Mini Book Will Get You Blessed, If You Do, What I Did with Excellence with Your Credit Profile Also!

T.h.u.g.g. family and supporters' times are getting really hard in our economy, and you need your credit score right for whets in the near future that we are about to experience.

Paper money is fading away, but your good credit and the word of God will sustain you through these hard times that are getting harder each passing month with mounting prices for food, gas, housing, and so on.

Don't get left out of the credit game when you can get your credit right today!

If this short book registers with you and you want to support this ministry, below is how you donate and give!

Give on our secure website for credit or debit card payments.

www.changedpeopletoday.org

We take Cash app donations at/$Thuggbishup that's a dollar sign/Thuggbishup

Checks or money orders must be written to this address.

Changed People Today.

P.O. BOX 18731

Saint Louis, MO.

63118

Office/314-925-8853

Email/info@changedpeopletoday.org

THUGGALUJAH!!!!!!!

THANKS IN ADVANCE FOR YOUR TIME AND FOCUS ON THIS SHORT STORY!

SINCERELY YOURS,

BISHUP AND SARAH AKUA RICH WEALTH!

Made in United States
North Haven, CT
04 November 2026

21769529R00015